INQUIRIES

INQUIRIES

p o e m s

MICHELLE PORTER

BREAKWATER
P.O. Box 2188, St. John's, NL, Canada, A1C 6E6
WWW.BREAKWATERBOOKS.COM

A CIP catalogue record for this book is available from Library and Archives Canada

ISBN 978-1-55081-792-8

We acknowledge the support of the Canada Council for the Arts. We acknowledge the financial support of the Government of Canada and the Government of Newfoundland and Labrador through the Department of Business, Tourism, Culture and Rural Development for our publishing activities.

PRINTED AND BOUND IN CANADA.

Canada Council for the Arts Conseil des Arts du Canada Canada Newfoundland Labrador

Breakwater Books is committed to choosing papers and materials for our books that help to protect our environment. To this end, this book is printed on a recycled paper and other controlled sources that are certified by the Forest Stewardship Council®.

For my Métis grandmothers,
who too often walked their paths alone.

For my First Nations ancestors, the grandmothers
who made the paths for us all to walk.

For my European grandmothers, the ancestors
who sometimes dared to leave the path given to them.

For my grandchildren, born and yet to be born:
you are the future of the path I walk.

For my mother. For the path you walked when I was a child
and the path you are still walking.

For my daughters, for the joy, laughter,
and friendship you've brought me.

Marsi

ACKNOWLEDGMENTS

I am grateful to ArtsNL for the financial support provided early in the life of this project.

Thank you to the editors of *Red Rising*, *Grain*, and *The Malahat Review* where earlier versions of some of these poems first appeared.

I am grateful to Katherena Vermette for the mentorship and support I received during the development of this manuscript. Your direct responses have been invaluable, and your kindness gave me courage.

Thank you to Maria Campbell for sharing insights about drawing from personal history in writing. Your warmth and wisdom showed me the way I needed to go.

I am grateful to Lee Maracle for being so generous with her advice and insights about writing from personal experience and the importance of writing memory in a direction that leads toward hope and humour. I learned so much from you over the course of a single evening.

Thank you to Rob Finley and Mary Dalton for seeing what my work could be and teaching me how to move a little farther in that direction.

Thank you to my sister, Colleen, for being there.

CONTENTS

OF THE RED

Here the river keens and calls
in the waning of the born

prairie light, and
I'm here you reply at last:

ma soeur, ma mère, my
heart, my bones, my blood.

Tomorrow the solstice will
finger-weave a fine sash

of a day, knotted tassels
offered to the shoulders

of the Red:
ma soeur, ma mère, my

heart, my bones, my blood.
You have been gone so long,

your silted days lived in exile, your
nights lost in the black fringe

of a continent's memory.
Only now you see how fertile the borders are,

the parallel banks of the Red's round, fat hips,
your first home, your river wet with belonging,

threading tight the thirsty land: ma soeur, ma
mère, my heart, my bones, my blood.

NORTH SASKATCHEWAN RIVER, 1980s

They waited for the roads to arrive and couldn't say where
the tributaries converged. Mama had to figure out how to merge

with transport trucks. They didn't know they could take their uncle's
canoe to the banks and paddle the silver current all the way to their

homelands, the travelling sun licking their edible backs. So Mama held her
breath
on Highway 216 and exited from Yellowhead East onto St. Albert Trail

Northwest and finally they were almost at their auntie's townhouse,
almost running
on her earth with their cousins, the seven boys growing at the bend in the road.

MAMA DOESN'T PRAY BUT SHE BUYS LOTTERY TICKETS: MAMA'S KITCHENS I

The kitchen can't stop talking   about
its single steam-punk window, retelling legends
about the crabapple tree outside,   spinning tales

to the picnic table, the tall wooden fence, gossiping
about the neighbours who pray on the other side.
The sink is held upright by linoleum, and   offers

the water blessing so Mama can perm his hair
in the three-bedroom duplex she can't afford to rent.
Were they there for a year? Hard to say. The children   watch.

Lace curtains pulled in place by yellow sashes and arranged
according to Bible verses. Below the window is the steel sink
where he lowers his head.

Mama doesn't pray but she buys lottery tickets, figures
the odds are better. When her numbers come up, Mama's going to quit
her job and live off the land, teach her kids to survive without the city

that wastes them. The children press and jostle
when Mama comes   home,
Mama doesn't bring friends, doesn't   touch

and now this man in this kitchen,   who calls
their mama's fingers into his hair, and they witness
deliverance, Jesus promises wearing snakeskin boots.

And the kitchen can't stop talking.

WHITEWAY STREET, 2008

All she ever says about it is she rented
the place by phone before they ever got

to the city. Never fought anyone before, not
like that. Did it for her kids. Swore

she'd call the health inspectors,
threatened til the landlord let her off the

lease. Knew she had him by the balls.

TESSIER PLACE, 2012-2014

When the old electric mixer broke,
she didn't buy a new one.

She was that broke.

Found a forty-cent whisk
at a yard sale, down the road some.

Told her kids how whipping cream by hand
tastes better.

THE JOINTS OF THE STORIES: MAMA'S KITCHENS II

Sometimes, she digs up
the joints
and sets them

in a roasting
pan and bakes them
with mushrooms.

Hours or days at a stretch,
in the length and the simmer of the kitchen. Sometimes,
when she isn't perming his hair

at the sink,
she'll shake stories
from her dark hair

and the children
will pick the meat off the bones.
One day, one day, she begins,

the fancy French relatives
come to the woods
looking to eat them all.

The kitchen cupboard
near bare. The fiddle on the chair,
the outhouse over there,

the sewing machine in the corner,
the wood stove a hibernating
bear, and seven half-breed

brothers and sisters who've misplaced
the stories created to save them.

OPEN A DOOR AND

–after Deanna Young's poem "If a Door Opened"

I.

They will pour outside, dragging garbage
bags filled with unfolded clothes and
resentment.

Think of the satisfied houses,
watching as they run, innards exhaled
into sneering yellow cabs.

II.

Shelter over capacity, kindness takes refuge in
a cheap room, the hotel bar hits on her again, she lies
still

for hours, smelling of bitter almonds. She has
never smoked in her shrinking life, only in
her dreams.

III.

What if we won? she asks. *Just one million?* Now
they gather round, talking fast, borrowing
fantasies.

A woman and her four
children: when they leave, someone sweeps up
the scratch tickets.

IV.

Must be fifty of them left behind,
on the floor, not one
a winner.

THIS HAUNTING

Fingers fumbling for the ghost
of a cigarette. My mother smoked Player's Light,
slim piano hands shaking each time the police were called.
Grandma smoked two packs a day, died

slowly in a hospital bed, gaunt eyes dreaming the French
and the Michif she'd misplaced. Mama said how Grandpa
took his family out of Manitoba back then, said he didn't
want to be treated like an Indian anymore. Mama's

cigarette, the dark smear of lipstick here, the grey ash glow
there. Ancestral memory, sleepless grief. I crave the ritual
I'd put aside: nervous tap between fingers,
aching throat, sacred twist of smoke. My mouth

recalls just what to do. The storm carried away consolation
but this ghost between my fingers, this wraith of
wanting, this fertile cigarette in hands that
never held one.

THE STARE OF MAMA'S MEN: MAMA'S KITCHENS III

There, on the edge
of the sink in the duplex,
she opens

two bulging boxes of pink and yellow
perm rods. Yarns of light cling to her fingers, and memories
of Grandmama carried out of the woods again, unconscious,

another lifetime ago. Doesn't know what year it is, does she?
She tells time by the fight in the stare of her
men. All that is left

is heavy bitumen. She curls it
into the crusade of her new boyfriend's hair, names it
hope. There: a small, tightly wound man

in expensive shit-kickers, blue jeans
hugging hard, narrow hips. A towel on the edge
of the sink to cradle the back of his neck.

HOME, 1985-1991

Tucked in the bed of a truck, lurching down the highway, limbs
knotted with the sky they call their Grandmother, who watches,

star eyes fierce, spilling half-moon gossip. Home is on the way
to somewhere else. The truck a house without a roof, the road

rushing ahead to our beginning.
Gaps between the stacked boxes and bed springs just large enough

for two girl children. The flat of a truck, listening to the squeak
of ball joints and the shudder of a mud flap on all-season tires.

Peanut butter and day-old bread. Every now and then, there are
fat drive-thru burgers and pink shakes. Their eyes on the horizon,

watching for places to stop.

SLICING LEMONS IN APRIL

Talk about moving away while a blizzard moves in. He chops sausage
and they try on plans: Back to Alberta? Maybe Manitoba,

where her people are from? Or should they find their way to Europe,
where he is from? Spicy chorizo in a cast-iron pan. Onions in hot oil

and the sharp scent of Spanish spice. BC is too much, isn't it?
Too expensive for them, right? In the second bathroom down the hallway

newly made photos of the mainland dry on a line. Would there be work
for them in Ontario? The next provincial budget is gonna cut both

their jobs, right? Though, maybe not. They could stick it out, couldn't
they? Now the blade slices through an Argentinian lemon, creating defiant

yellow wheels that are riddles in this April snowstorm. A can of solid,
dependable
chickpeas shipped to the island from Iran. Cracking eggs now. Orange orbs
gaping

in the pan. Ground pepper. The oven door squeaks shut. Ten minutes. He sits
to read aloud to her. Something about how ordinary wasn't supposed to
happen

to people like the writer, come from nothing. The words aren't the thing for her.
It's the sound of his voice and the mug she grips in her hands. It's the dinner

that will come swearing hot from the oven in ten minutes, and it's the children
about
to leave their crayons and paper, children who will rush to the table when
called.

CARTONS OF MILK HOLD EVERYTHING UP: MAMA'S KITCHENS IV

The spider on the web in the kitchen window held back by
yellow sashes drinks   its own sentences from a husk while
the milkman outside steps from concrete tile to concrete

tile, toward the front door, holding a crate of milk products in
his arms,   an offering. With this work he pays for
title to the lawn he waters and mows every two days

and rationalizes the house built on a prairie that cradles
trails no one's followed for decades,
on land always offering

its generous, aching grasses
to moving seas of murmuring
hooves pushed out by inflation and housing bubbles.

His name is Jean-Louis, Mama told the children,
the night she brought him home: not the milkman,
the new man. The older sister married them quickly that night,

the Bible heavy in her growing hands. Now Mama hauls
the refrigerator door open all the time just to look
over the last delivery. Cartons of milk are sturdy

and there's never powder or lumps and not so much shame.
The spider bends over the milkman's bill weekly, and Mama
counts the concrete tiles the milkman walks before she pays.

MÉTIS MOTHER RETURNING FROM THE GROCERY STORE, ALBERTA

You know when the plastic cuts into her piano fingers and the weight
of food for four children makes her elbows ache, she scrapes the bus fare

from the lining of her purse and you wait with her at the sign as the sun beads
the sweat on your foreheads so you won't forget who you are even

though you don't speak the language, and then the clank of change, the walk
between seats, the quick step over the narrow lilting floor, mimicking Mama's

rhythms as she counters the thrusting start-stop and the squelching open-close
of the bus's lead, and seeing what Mama sees so when you find

a seat and look out her window there is the caw of traffic and the bear of engine,
and the quiet of green banks listening to a gush of water,

and right here at the intersection your mama shows you a gathering of grand
trees, gnarly with the world's anguish and gossiping to hold the world together,

and at your concrete stop you try to carry as many bags as you can to give
her a rest and
you walk to the unnatural heat of the apartment and put the groceries away,
count

the number of days you'll eat and she just wants coffee and a cigarette, to
take a break
from creating the world, and you are there but also still on the bus, travelling
upright

on torn and faded vinyl, borrowing her eyes to see places you've never been,
holding stories you've never lived, grafting futures not meant to be yours.

IN THE CITY, ALBERTA

Mama dreamed the bush into every city we moved to because Mama
could. The mayors believed Mama disinherited them. That's why they said those

things. Mama converted exhaust's erotic obsession into a shaded nest of
nightjars
with the twisting sort of flight everyone remembered they'd been looking for all
along,

a sort of aching that bankrupted their family picnics and cancelled their
cheques.
Those poor children, they said of us, and they told their descendants not to
let us eat

cake or potato chips at their parties. Because Mama had something and
everyone
could see it, because Mama dreamed the bush into all the cities we walked.

TO THE LAST CENT: MAMA'S KITCHENS V

No downcast gaze,
her, she looks a man
in the eye, throwing

carbonized high-calibre
signals until he wants her
more than his next meal,

more than his own
sharp self. All she owns
is the distance between tables,

the long hours, the high
heels, and the feet
sore to breaking. Limps home most nights

to sit still in the kitchen and listen to the sleep
of the children, but she damn well pays the milk bill,
to the last cent, and on time.

THE Es

In school each student had to
write a poem about their mother.
She wrote "my friend

and my foe" with the Es
finally facing the right way. On
the way home, she wondered

which mother would be waiting.

THE JUMP OF HER FEET

One day she was called to the
office. Her mom sat there, smile

in the right place.

Get your stuff, honey. We're going.

What?

Hurry. Say goodbye if you want to,
but be quick. He's out in the truck,
with the rest.

She was the new kid, just getting
skinny calf legs beneath her, figuring
which girls to stay away from.

We're moving, she whispered
to the girl who asked as she
grabbed her bag and pencil case.

From the covered cab of the truck,
she watched the school turn
a corner and she thought how

she'd left her gym shoes in
the change room with the
others, how the jump of her

feet and the tie of her laces
would always be there.

THE HUNGRY END OF THE MONTH: MAMA'S KITCHENS VI

The lusty late-night slice of hot bread
kitchen, the margarine melting and tied apron
kitchen. The anxious kitchen, the hungry end of the month kitchen, the worried
half-loaf

kitchen. The skinny handful of potatoes kitchen, the greedy scarce cup of sugar
kitchen. The last scrape of peanut butter shared between five kitchen.
The windowless kitchen, the overheated withdrawal from antidepressants
kitchen.

The low-income kitchen. The welfare kitchen. The kitchen of her daydreams,
with bright bursting cupboards and clean floors. The white kitchen. The
sitcom
kitchen. The kitchen she conjures when she's scanning classifieds

before the next move, the blowing her last twenty on scratch tickets kitchen.
The gutted kitchen. The empty
except for cardboard boxes kitchen. The last

wipe of the fridge before the final truck-load kitchen.
The kitchen at the end of the road. The kitchen always
about to be hers and the kitchen she'll never see again.

FEAST DAY

Younger sister cradles a handful of potatoes as she descends
the narrow, carpeted stairs, penitent. *I was hungry*,

she tells everyone, but she's not offering an excuse, no
she's confessing a weakness, how the body betrays the

spirit every time, how her own flesh had led her to the
sin of greed, a girl hoarding the family's last ten potatoes,

stolen out of the kitchen cupboard after everyone knew
there would be no more potatoes coming home

from the store. She hid them under her bed in a plastic bag—take
one out when the half-dozen ten-cent buns shared between

five were not enough, eat one entire potato whole and raw in the secret of
the night. She descends now, when there is no food left downstairs,

the uneaten earth apples spilling from her arms, Lord keep
us all from temptation. *I can't keep these for myself*, she says, and

she is broken by the need of her own belly. God, but doesn't she
make her sister laugh? Until the tears roll down

their cheeks, until they drape their arms around each other's
shoulders, until one of them gasps something about baking.

The miracle of the oven, transforming perfect guilt
into rich starch: soft, fleshy, and weak.

THE FRIDGE THINKS ABOUT MOVING OUT

Before they moved in, the fridge lived
another life, went dancing
until 4 a.m., came home
passed out in the middle of

the kitchen floor,
couldn't remember who left the steaks,
the sauces, the poultry, and the grapes.

Before they moved in, the fridge
had never touched secondhand clothes,
overdue pastries or foodbank cans.

In its youth, the fridge was quite a player,
polyamorous: no responsibilities, no children,
no long-term expectations.

Children expect things,
the fridge will tell you that,
even when they learn to expect nothing
you can see it in their faces,
the low-wattage bulbs
that light up when any door opens a crack.

Now, even when the fridge is stoned or hungover
or aching from withdrawal,
even when the fridge creaks
with osteoarthritis,
there's that damn light,
like it or not.

The fridge sleeps most afternoons now
and paces hallways at night,

listening for the ugly silence,
the kids coughing, or the shabby
arguments between the mother and boyfriend.
The fridge worries.
It can't eat a proper meal.

The fridge sucks on the crusts of bread
dropped on the floor, not picked up for days.

It keeps near-empty ketchup bottles,
stores bruised apples—
no more than one per day per child,
or they won't last three days, will they?

The fridge would like to kick them out,
thinks it could pull itself together again for a
professional couple with good jobs,
a regular sex life and no need for budgets.

The fridge thinks about moving out,
but sometimes these flickering kids,
they look in and find the yogurt
the fridge scrimped for days to buy,
or a block of cheddar the fridge found on discount,
jealously measured so no one gets more as
they salivate over the obscene luxury
of a grilled cheese.

The fridge
knows it can't leave,
it can't go on with its life,
not until the children are fed.

CARRY BREAD CRUMBS: MAMA'S KITCHENS VII

to cradle

He arrived at the kitchen door,
a traveller from the east.

the back of his neck

The children didn't know which fairy tale
they were playing.

tight brown curls
the tap open and running

Brought him home
with her tips one crowded night,
said: *he's moving in with us.*

a towel on the edge
of the sink, she

Carry bread crumbs. Look for his shadow. Watch for the pointed ears
folded beneath his curls. Check the temperature with bony fingers.
Guide his head under the tap.

works her fingers
through his hair.

WAITING TO GO

Here at the door, unravel the plans she's made so many times
before. Always leaving, never going. Hand twitchy on the knob, knowing

she'll find one more delay. Now, right here, the storms within
are growing larger than the thing that rattles the hinges from out there:

always leaving, never going. Determination folds, she gapes at
people passing on the street. Maybe today? No, not today. So many times

here at the door, pacing, clammy with the heat of her impatience. She
should quit this house for good. Today? Just walk, just creep, away.

Now? No, not today. So many times shrieking, shrieking at the door,
knowing, always leaving, never going.

MILLWOODS, EDMONTON

Annexation crowds in with them there, where their mama's brother
watches over them so she can go to the river in search of a new

father and where he slips giant lollipops under their pillows at night to
make up for the fish they will never eat. They'd forgotten there was

a long tradition of stealing the land because they walk everywhere,
and that is what ties the treaties tight to the houses, what grows

the grass taller than they stand, what asks the rain to make the mud
that pools beneath the swings and cools their bare feet. They don't

know how to see the Papaschase people and they can't see themselves,
but who is singing the rhythm when they skip rope and who listens to

their mama's stories about creatures living in the heating vents, the
ones who steal children, one by one, to keep them beneath the earth.

FROM THE BONES OF THIS STORY: MAMA'S KITCHENS VIII

Grandmama builds

some kind of soup

from the bones
of this history:

Withered this, scrap of that.
Wasn't much else to cook for the rich relatives
come by to rub it in, with salt.

You get what you deserve.

A startle of soup from a wood-stove kitchen because they can't eat a crooked phrase.

Disinherited.

The smell fills the shivering house.

ELDERING

She is eldering. It is time for her to fall. This will not
wait. She drinks from the river at her roots because those waters

have not stopped moving, not once, and this gives her courage.
She is eldering now. It is time for her

to fall. This will not wait. She will have to unbranch. Her trunk is sugaring
for the season to come. She is eldering now. She is

going to fall. She is still part summer and she holds the sap
from the spring that created her. The time of telling is on the way

and she must learn the stories asking for her voice. She is
eldering now. She will fall. This will not wait. She is afraid.

She cannot withstand the coming tectonic shift. There was not time enough to gather
what is needed for the approaching Cambrian night because she sat too many hours

in ergonomic office chairs. Her roots have been torn out of their earth.
She will have to be enough because it is time to carry others. The grandchildren

will take her hand. She is eldering. It is time. She is
falling. This will not wait. This will not wait.

THE TULIPS (ON MY COUNTER) ARE DYING

You are drunk women, retching and grasping
The rim of your lives with leaf fingernails.

Shocked by the massacre in your petals,
They told you "it gets better"—

And did that platitude carry your suffering
for you? Your water carried in the palms of those

Who shaped and picked you for their pleasure?
"It gets better" wasn't yours, was it? Not

With your straight stems, your three-chambered
Secrets, your darkening ovaries. Though, of course,

You repeated it to yourselves, didn't you? You whispered
"It gets better" to yourselves as you held your breath

For pruning, keeping still as a corpse for cutting,
Confessing your doubts with the shudder of packing,

Praying through the crackle of delivery, and dying with the sudden
Descent into cold, clear water. No bulb anymore,

Nothing to hold you upright in this world.
"It gets better" means nothing to you now, does it?

And why should it? Six petals, six sepals,
Six stamens, one flaccid pistil, and a loose, lippy

Three-lobed stigma. You dream of the dirt that gripped
Your feet while you were still part earth. For you,

It does not get better, it will not get better, not
For drunken tulips, leaning over a plastic palisade, not for you.

THE MÉTIS CHILDREN LEAN IN: MAMA'S KITCHENS IX

Grandpa releases a bedroom door from its old hinges and hauls it
on his shoulder down the stairs. He sets the door on four

crates, balances the door in the middle of the kitchen floor. There, he says,
a table big enough for us all. The children lean in

when Mama gets to this part of the story. The door
is not in its proper place so the story can't end,

not like this. The door no longer opens to witness feet
moving down the hallway,

no longer grants access
from one way of life to another. The door is a riddle. It can't

keep anything out, not anymore.
Sip my wife's soup, says Grandfather, sit at my door.

MARCH 14, 2014

The man next door was beaten to death
with a baseball bat while I

set out the Playmobil house on the floor
for a couple of four year olds

who wore pink, gauzy wings.
The Curious George soundtrack was playing,

so we didn't hear any screams, nothing.
Proper two-storey, three-bedroom

doll house, it was. We set the toy mom
in its plastic yard to pick up the needles.

THE WIRE ON TESSIER PLACE

Everybody was watching
The Wire that year,

remember? We had to quit.
That shit was too real. If we

wanted to know what happened to a street
overrun by dealers, only had to sit out

on the stoop. Watch season one live,
in real time and up close.

LIKE JESUS, THE SKY LOVES THE LITTLE CHILDREN: MAMA'S KITCHENS X

Mama listens to the preacher who comes
to her door. Just in case, she thinks, and
she sends her children to be fed in church

Like Jesus, the sky loves the little children and,

basement kitchens on Sundays with the ladies
who organize prayer potlucks on white stoves
and sing so hard at God they sweat dark stains

beneath the sky, the land. Renovates ideas of
kitchens, tells stories of campfires. The fridge, the
stove, the sink: they stay behind, cloistered in their
safe houses, can't get near your bones, can't steal
your gossip. Even in the city there's fire pits where,

through their good dresses, singing always
makes for glad hearts, yes, but the children fidget, wait
to leave, search with their eyes for windows, where

the mothers gather to escape the mean antics
of walls and narrowness of bored rooms, offer
hot dogs and marshmallows to the cousins.

the aunts wrap chicken legs and onion in tinfoil, let the fire
char and scorch. The sky bleeds out, settles like a blanket.
Night gentles their talk and pokes the fire. Sparks rise, vanish.

PICKING UP THE BABY

Babies are manipulative, they'll cry but you've got to show them
you won't crack, who's boss. So she gets them all sleeping through

the night at three months. She likes to say it's because of the book they
learn not to call for what they need from the world. When the crying

brings grandma crashing through the door of the basement apartment
below her music house—the buried shelter she offers her

children—Mama knows it's time to be moving on. She knows it's time to make
her own way in the world, to raise her babies the new way. She witnesses

Grandma undo all the hours of leaving her first son to cry, of teaching
him that his parents are stronger than his hunger. Grandma ruins it by

picking up the squalling brat, cradling him and crooning: *it's all right, I'm here,*
right here, before turning her face to Mama's, brown eyes rich with accusation.

COLONIAL STREET, 2009

Must have baked hundreds of batches of cookies
in that galley kitchen, while

the two year old and the six year old mucked about
out back. Neighbour warned her,

said there's lead in that dirt.
But what could she do?

Wash their hands when they came in.

THE FAUCET WOULD LIKE TO SIT DRY: MAMA'S KITCHENS XI

The door is set on four crates. The sink
wants to finish, to get rid of
the coming story. The door is in the middle.
The faucet is always pouring. The door is
in a story. The faucet would like to amend
its water. The door cannot let anyone through.
The door shuts the family into being.
The sink wants the plug. The door remembers the future
when one of the children grows into a mother of five
trembling over a hard-times Métis man who wants
a woman to perm his hair. The door turns into
a table and they set the large pot of soup on its
back because stories are like that. The faucet
would like to sit dry, without pouring.

MANOLIS L OFF DUCK ISLAND, NOTRE DAME BAY

There's this cofferdam between us and disaster. Eight tanks
of oil in a wreck in the North Atlantic. Lord—the hull is cracked

and it's leaking faster. Sweet Jesus, we can apply neoprene
like plaster. We can drop sand bags over every leak and nick, but

there's only a cofferdam between us and disaster. Heavy fuel oil
and growlers give to no master. And the holding tank walls aren't

all that thick. Dear God—the hull is cracked and it's leaking faster.
Five-hundred-thousand litres and a sou'wester. Don't panic, sure

there's a cofferdam between us and disaster. Could we pull
the wreck out before storms batter? They'll investigate the options,

frantic. Lord—the hull is cracked and it's leaking faster. There's
resistance to flow, say the forecasters, and considering the structural

condition of the ship, there's just this cofferdam between us and disaster.
God help us—the hull is cracked and it's leaking faster, faster.

THE MORNING AFTER

–after Lisa Bird-Wilson's short story "Counselling"

Were you wearing a condom
last night? I'm empty.

You know I want
to fill up on other people.
I'm empty.

The condom: I looked
this morning before I left
you sleeping.

The people I love
nothing but ghosts, they
disappear.

You know, I want
to be full
of people.

You know, I have family
all over the prairies
I've never met.

Anyway, I didn't see
any signs of a condom,
no open wrappers.

Love is a perfect marble
I stole from your house
when your back was turned.

So many beautiful things
all your life. What's
one glass marble to you?

No silicone sheath, sticky
on the floor beside the bed,
nothing in the garbage bin.

Only what I steal is mine.

THE FRIDGE IS AN ATHEIST: MAMA'S KITCHENS XII

His head under the faucet, Mama working her fingers through
tight curls. Perm rods flash yellow and pink between long,

slim fingers. Wrapping hair in slips of paper and attaching
the rod end. Wrapping, attaching.

Her hands slow at his neck.
The children pull at their naked tangles in awe:

their mama doesn't touch. They know
the nights are on their way, when they will not sleep

for clutching kitchen knives and prayers against
Mama's spit and his rosary of threats, against the slam

of the door behind him. Love is the tradition of his return
in the capitulation of light, three days later,

love is milk, a born-again kitchen, an atheist fridge,
full bellies paid for, receipt in hand. Waiting for the perm to set.

Waiting with a towel around his shoulders
to keep the drip from his shirt.

LEAVING CALGARY

Almost didn't make it out of hibernation that year but
a nagging drip, an early melt, found its way in before spring

and woke us. What you leave behind never stays where
you left it. It was the dollhouse Mama talked about

for years, the one we didn't have room for in the
station wagon. Taller than me, with a serene

elevator and untroubled plastic furniture. She knew I'd
be near grown before she could afford to buy another.

The sun hurt my eyes when we drove away,
the imprint of home still pressed into my cheek.

IF THE TABLE HAD BEEN STRONGER

Mama fell and turned the tables.
She wanted to belong to us, but
Mama lied and fed us fables.

Legs and arms were strong and able,
She could have been our safe house—but
Mama fell and turned the tables.

Mama's telling rocked our cradles.
Our tales might have been longer, but
Mama lied and she fed us fables.

Here, our lives birthed through betrayal—
She believed she could belong to us.
Mama fell and turned the tables.

We wanted her to hold us stable.
Once upon and long ago.
Mama fell and turned the tables—
How Mama lied, how she fed us fables.

MARINATE THE BONES: MAMA'S KITCHENS XIII

The pot of soup was heavy, kicking,
and pregnant. The crates that held the tabletop

were unsteady. The table tipped and the pot fell.
The soup spread across the plank kitchen floor.

The pot of soup was heavy and pregnant.
The soup spilled into the rest of her life, marinating.

The table tipped and the pot fell. The crates were
unsteady. Marinating the bones of her stories.

PACKING BOXES AND LOADING THE TRUCK

I will not carry your grief on my hip, will not
wet this husk of guilt because the time has come
to leave. I will be your homecoming, here, there.

I will not bury my uterus in this silted river to keep you
from the future. You will miss the land you once belonged to
when you learn to crack the sun's marrow and listen for

gristle in the stories.
The land of your birth will settle, become your spine.
Leave the remains of these lives

for the ones who will rush in when we turn our backs.
Child, loss must sharpen
your reflexes. Your soles will callous
and the earth will corroborate your leaving.

PILLAR OF SALT

That other life where you belong.
Beneath a rutting, sweating light, you wake slow
With your tribe of good times and all night long.
And even if your hands were shaking so
You couldn't hold a moaning needle still
You held each other's arms and tracks
And stroked the bulging veins, until
The shaft went in and all went slack, and
You lay pissing against the wall.

That other life, where you were king
Of the score, the smoke, the stumble and sprawl,
And you kissed and you pissed against the wall. The only thing
What keeps you here is your kid, that pillar of salt,
Your bit of green, that weed pressing through tar and asphalt.

WHERE THE SONGS ROOT AND GROW: MAMA'S KITCHENS XIV

When the stories won't stop
telling themselves she walks

from the old plank-floored house
out the front door

to the bush where the songs
root and grow, to her circle

of trees, and there she pulls
dead branches to mark

the make-believe kitchen
she never really leaves.

A branch for a broom
and earth between the roots

home: this gathering of trees,
the sound silence makes

from the rustle of living things, a little girl
sweeping the soft earth with a boney branch.

HOME, 2017, KING'S ROAD

No curtains
in the kitchen, even
after two years.

Never know when
she might be moving
on.

But she gets a craving
for every bit of
light that
comes through
those windows.

Can't get enough.

Lord knows, there's
not a spare drop of sun,
not a scrap to waste,
not here.

THE SOUTH SASKATCHEWAN, JULY 2018

Night will stalk the trail to this valley and I will go down to the river behind the house I do not belong to. The teenagers in the water will splash like children and laugh like men, come from the reserve up the way, or maybe they will be Métis, come here for Batoche, like me. On my face I wear provisional pink skin and white mineral sunblock. This avalanche of sun burned my hair blonde. I will watch the shining children pile into their cars and drive away. I will squat and offer both hands to the rush of the river so I can share her tributaries and be introduced to her fish. I will tell her my story: *my great-grandfather did not swim here, he shed his scales and passed over this earth for what he could buy in British Columbia with money from selling a paper scrip promise, five acres for himself and five for each daughter*. The South Saskatchewan River will welcome me and I will take off my shoes. I will say: *my great-grandfather dragged trees from the forest that he owned by legal contract and sold the logs to feed his family. This was the price he agreed to pay for the fiddling and the jigging he could not leave by the Red River*. When the woman in the house up the road stands, her head is the sky. She has invited me in. I want to say: *I am someone's granddaughter; A white-skinned Métis grown in the city; My mother's stories were the milk that kept me from hunger on days we didn't eat; Her stories fed my bones so they became hollow and light*. The woman in the white house wrote histories I recognized and hid away for the days of empty cupboards. I will take nothing from the river because my grandfather never spawned here. I will walk past the white house I do not belong to and I will get into my car. Daylight will pack up, and evening will arrive, and the South Saskatchewan will watch my back as I drive away. Her stare will ache in my joints.

THE TIME COMES

How dying whitens your branches, draws the eye.
Lit with the memory of death, and the future

Of life.
How it sculpts your bones, even as

Spring swells the buds that still come eager
And natural to your brown branches.

It is spring and you continue to lean
Into the rest of your life.

Nouhkom—
When the time comes, I will cry

Because you showed me dying is a celebration
And I always cry when I am happy.

ARE YOU HUNGRY?: MAMA'S KITCHENS XV

Thirty-five below zero that day and no one is home so
they knock on the door on the left side of the duplex. A woman

opens her door to the frozen children who have come from school.
She wears a broom skirt, and the baby on her hip babbles. Her husband

is at work, but his guitar stands in the corner. She rubs the children's stinging fingers,
checks their toes. The garden they watched her grow through the gaps in the fence the past

summer is buried under drifts. Somewhere in St. Albert is a duplex where
the kitchen can't stop talking about its one window, retelling legends about

a tree, spinning tales to the picnic table and the tall wooden fence, gossiping
about the neighbours who pray on the right side and about their steel sink.

There's a crabapple tree sleeping there just out the window near the fence they aren't
allowed to cross. Are you hungry, the mother from the left side asks? They nod.

FOUR NIGHTS AT A BED AND BREAKFAST, WALDHEIM

The very next day you're up and in the garden
with the glistening webs. The very next day the sun

pulls the blood into each green berry, ripening. Thirteen
when you last did this, weren't you? Riding bicycle

along the backroads to the farm by yourself. Your days
ribboning along in the pulsing heat, and the raspberries

ripe and tender as life in your open hand.
The sky gives up its gregarious performance

and turns its back so you put one sticky berry
into your mouth, just one,

because loving is reckless and can poison you. You don't know
where you are, do you? The berries are histories that were tacked

to the bushes before you arrived, and so you wait before you reach for one
more, because remembering is treacherous and can maim you. The berry is wet

and cool on the bush, soft with readiness. The berry wants to leave the stem
now so you do what it asks, you pull it away from the only

home it has known. You wonder if it hurts, this dismemberment.
In your mouth the berry falls apart on your tongue. It doesn't

taste like it did back then. Of course it doesn't. You are not that child
anymore. You have lived through calendars of sunless days, gripped

cliffs that offered only gales as compensation for the life
to be lived. The berry falls apart on your tongue. Taste

its tart ache. You swallow. Now there is sun in your belly and you carry
this away, a memory that will not shatter, not shard.

COLONIAL STREET, 2010

The roof leaked.
Hell, the walls

leaked when wind blew the rain
sideways.

Just the way roofs are
in Newfoundland,

said her landlady. Just
the way it is.

MAMA IN THE WINDOW: MAMA'S KITCHENS XVI

Mama haunting the window. Long, black hair.
She glances through and slips away.

A woman haunting. Where is the milkman?
She materializes.

Were they there for a year? They can't
put this time together in one soup,

can't sew it into a dress, with the first
stitch here and the last there. The kitchen

can't stop talking. The window, waiting.
She slips away.

The bill is due. She glances through the window.
The milkman?

CHILDHOOD, REMEMBERED

as a girl
she could turn into a river.

when she wanted to get away from here
and go there, she only had to lay down

and lean into the easiest route.
the going and arriving happened all at once—

she was always tumbling down rocks and cliffs
beneath the slant of the sun at the same time as she

pooled, still as a mountain, at the place she never, ever
finished going to.

Michelle Porter is a citizen of the Métis Nation and member of the Manitoba Metis Federation, and has called Newfoundland and Labrador home for almost ten years now. She is currently the non-fiction editor with *Riddle Fence* and is studying creative writing and teaching journalism. Porter holds a BA in Journalism and Communications, an MA in Folklore, and a PhD in Geography. In both 2016 and 2017, her work was longlisted for the CBC Poetry Prize. She lives in St. John's.